I0422875

# Dolphins
# For Kids

# Amazing Animals Books for
# Young Readers

**by Natalia Asfar**
**Mendon Cottage Books**

*JD-Biz Publishing*

## Download Free Books!
## http://MendonCottageBooks.com

All Rights Reserved.
No part of this publication may be reproduced in any form or by any means, including scanning, photocopying, or otherwise without prior written permission from JD-Biz Corp and http://AmazingAnimalBooks.com. Copyright © 2015

All Images Licensed by Fotolia and 123RF

**Read More Amazing Animal Books**

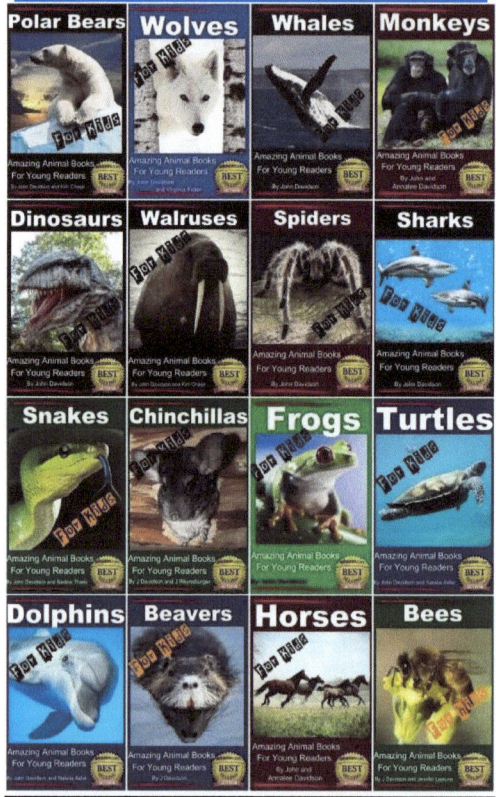

**Purchase at Amazon.com**

**Download Free Books!**
**http://MendonCottageBooks.com**

# Table of Contents

# 1. Introduction to Dolphins

*Dolphins are very smart animals, they are found worldwide, mostly in shallow seas and oceans. Dolphins love to eat fish and squid. Dolphin's colors are all different. No two dolphins are the same. The colors vary greatly, but they are generally gray in color with darker backs than the rest of their bodies.*

Dolphins are well known to be friendly and calm but they LOVE to play.

You will be surprised if you know that:

- Dolphins are mammals; this means that they nurse their babies with milk from the mothers.

- Dolphins can swim up to 300 meters below the surface of the ocean.

- Dolphins can stay up to 15 minutes under water, but they cannot breathe under the water.

- Dolphins communicate and talk through making sounds and whistles.

All this and many other interesting facts you will learn when you read this book.

## 2. 10 Facts about Dolphins

1. Dolphins do not sleep fully because they need to be awake in order to breath or else they will suffocate.

2. Dolphins can be dangerous when provoked. You should therefore avoid provoking them. Otherwise they are very friendly to human beings.

3. An adult dolphin eats about 250kg of food per day. This is equivalent to 9 percent of its total body weight.

4. Dolphins are very good divers. For example, they can dive down to 300 meters.

5. The average lifespan of a dolphin is about 20 years. This means that after reaching twenty years of age, it dies.

6. A dolphin usually does not live alone but live in groups called pods. A pod is comprised of up to 1, 0000 dolphins.

7. Dolphins are similar to porpoises but dolphins have rounded interlocking teeth while porpoises have squared teeth.

8. When a dolphin is born, it has to swim to the water surface to take its first breath.

9. Dolphins have excellent sense of hearing and eyesight.

10. There is a total of 67 species of dolphins. The largest specie is called orca or killer whale

# 3. What Do You Know About Dolphins

Dolphins are water mammals. Mammals mean that they drink milk from there mama.  They live in the sea and deep waters except for the very cold water because dolphins can't live in cold waters.

Dolphins love to swim in deep waters so you hardly ever see them near shores.

*© Andriy Bezuglov - Fotolia.com*

The total length of the normal dolphin is about 2.6 meters, and weighs about 140 kg, male dolphins are usually bigger than the female.

The colors vary and dolphins are very friendly and nice animals.

Dolphins have from 30 to 50 teeth, on each side of the jaw, but they don't bite people, they use their teeth to eat fish.

Dolphins are usually very peaceful and kind, they don't hurt people.

Some dolphins even learn how to do tricks for trainers. They are very smart and love people once they get to know them. At first they are very shy and scared. But after spending time with them and feeding them, they will do anything for a fish!

# 4. Types of Dolphins

There are 36 different types of dolphins, 32 marine and 4 types of dolphins which live in very large rivers.

The babies are called calves and the mamas are called dolphins. The males are called bulls and when they swim together in a bunch, they are called a pool or a pod.

© anilah - Fotolia.com

# 5. How Dolphins Come to Life

Baby dolphins stay in their mother's stomach for a very long time. They enter into this world after about eleven to eighteen months. At birth a calf is 33 to 55 inches long and almost 65 pounds. The baby calves stay with their mama for a very long time. They don't learn to hunt until they are about 6 years old.

*© petrock - Fotolia.com*

# 6. Why Dolphins Live in Water

Dolphins can breathe in water but I bet you didn't know that they can breathe outside of water on earth, too!

Well first because they don't have legs to walk, and even don't have wings to fly, so they can only swim.

Another thing, dolphins eat fish, and fish can only be found in the water, so dolphins live near their food.

*© Colette - Fotolia.com*

# 7. Dolphins Traveling in Water

From their very childhood dolphins swim, play, dance and travel in water. So naturally they become experts early in and above the water. They love to travel in water with groups. Traveling is the vital part of a dolphins culture and living.

Dolphins love to travel in groups in the water and swim in the waves. They love leaping above the water and doing flips!

Dolphins like warm water, so when winter comes, they travel together in groups to warmer places in the ocean.

*© Angelo Giampiccolo - Fotolia.com*

## 8. How Dolphins Breathe

Even though dolphins are a mammal, they need to breathe just like people do and all the other animals on earth. There is a hole on top of its head where they blow water out and when they dive, they close their hole up so water doesn't come in. They can hold their breathe for up to 15 minutes without breathing or coming up for air. That's probably when you see them come up to the surface and do flips and jump and play!

*© Kerri McClellan - Fotolia.com*

# 9. Dolphins Can Smell and See

*© Gennadiy Poznyakov - Fotolia.com*

Dolphins can smell and they can see.

Dolphins have very good eyesight. They need this to be able to protect themselves from predators lurking in the sea water.

Studies show that dolphins have excellent hearing as well. Dolphins ears are very small openings but don't let that fool you. They are also able to hear well under the water and it is due to them doing so through the lower jaw rather than only using the ears.

The lower jaw is able to conduct sound to the middle ear through a cavity that is filled with fat.

Even though dolphins can smell and see, they cannot taste.

# 10. What Dolphins Eat

Different types of dolphins eat different types of foods.

Dolphins use herding by swimming along in the ocean and eating the fish at the same time, by working together, like gathering a herd of cattle into the pastures.

*© Matthew Cole - Fotolia.com*

In addition to hunting in groups  dolphins are also able to hunt for food using echolocation which allows them to create sound waves and detect fish and other objects by what they hear when the echo comes back to them. Isn't that cool?

# 11. Dolphins Live With Family

Dolphins love their families. They also travel with their family and other dolphins and this group of dolphins is called a school. There often are as many as 100's but it is common to see about 12 or so as well doing flips out in the ocean. It is such a beautiful sight and so calming to see them swimming.

*© Angelo Giampiccolo - Fotolia.com*

# 12. Dolphins Can Be Your Friends

*© Maxim Larin - Fotolia.com*

Dolphins are curious sea creatures. They aren't like those mean sharks.

Instead, dolphins are like best friends. They help you when you're in need of help.

If you ever see a dolphin swimming in the sea, or in the pool, don't be afraid to play with it.

Dolphins are very kind, and they will love to play with you, even if you don't have a fish to feed them, you can touch them, and they will feel happy.

Yes, dolphins can be your friends they will never hurt you, as long as you are friendly with them.

But if you are swimming in the sea and playing with a dolphin, it will swim with you, and you will be the happiest kid ever.

# 13. Dolphins Play in Water

Dolphins spend a good portion of each day playing. They are great swimmers and enjoy leaping out of the water and doing somersaults in the air. They also enjoy catching the waves.

Surfers have reported seeing dolphins body surfing in the waves next to them. Dolphins will often seize the opportunity to enjoy swimming in the bow waves produced by boats.

© Tatjana Keisa - Fotolia.com

Dolphins can potentially find fun in playing with anything they find: Seaweed, coral, fish, trash or anything else a dolphin finds has the potential to become the object of their play. Dolphins have been observed in the wild playing games of catch.

Sometimes dolphins decide to play with other fish and mammals in the ocean; even if those other fish or mammals don't seem to want to play. Turtles, sea birds and fish have all become the objects of amusement for dolphins.

# 14. Dolphins Sleep Too

Like any mammal, the dolphin must sleep.

Dolphins sleep by resting one half of their brain at a time.
This means that one side of the dolphin's brain is "awake" while the other is in a deep sleep.

© *Lynne Nicholson - Fotolia.com*

This way of sleeping is very important to dolphins, not only because it helps dolphins to wake up when they need to breath, but also because this way it protects dolphins from any fish that may want to hurt them, and keeps the dolphins warm.

A common way that dolphins sleep is to swim very slowly along the surface, hardly moving, which allows them to continue breathing.

They typically close one eye, and although this does not always coordinate with which particular side of the brain stays alert, it does coordinate with their partner's open eye. Usually the two open eyes are looking at each other. If the dolphins switch positions, they also change which eye each has open. This type of sleeping behavior is called "rest swimming" or "logging." It is common in wild dolphins, and usually associated with calm water.

# 15. What Threatens Dolphins?

*© Andrey Armyagov - Fotolia.com*

There are many things that can harm dolphins or even kill them, let's see what they are:

- climate change : Like we said before dolphins like warm water, they can't live in cold water so when the weather becomes cold they travel, but some dolphins can't travel with others, and cold climate hurts them.

- Population : As you know the population (number of people) is growing and increasing very fast now, all the people need food, so to get more food for people some dolphins get killed by the fishing industry.

- Another is big fish: Like sharks, they can kill dolphins to eat.

- Pollution : Enormous amounts of waste products enter the sea, like plastic bags and dolphins eat them by mistake and this can cause harm.

# 16. People Can Harm Dolphins

Dolphins are very playful. They love to ride waves and do acrobatic stunts. That's why some of them are taken into the zoo to be trained. In spite of those qualities, we tend to hurt them unintentionally. Some people kill them for food. Some just cut them when they are entangled to their fishing nets. Others just catch too many fish leaving little for them to eat. But what kills them most is the pollution. People often visit their habitat and leave litter there.

© anilah - Fotolia.com

You may not know that you help in killing them by throwing garbage where it is not supposed to be. Because garbage on land and garbage that goes down the drain goes to the water they live in. Pollution is slowly killing them.

If you are trapped in a house that was dirty and no food was to be found in there, how would you feel? What you feel is what the dolphins feel.

The dolphins are affected by their surroundings, so we shouldn't hurt them by polluting the water and land as well, because like them one day we will suffer from the bad effects of pollution.

# 17. Rare Dolphins

*© tazzymon - Fotolia.com*

There are many types of dolphins which you can find in seas and oceans, but there are also some rare kinds which are very hard to find.

In the last 4 years people found 23 new kinds of dolphins, but because dolphins are scared of people they always swim away from researchers.

Hectore Dolphins: They are very rare, and considered to be the smallest dolphins.

River Dolphins : Only 4 kinds of dolphins being able to survive in freshwater

Risso's Dolphin: They are unique in how they look and so they are very appealing to both the common observer and to researchers.

**Download Free Books!**
**http://MendonCottageBooks.com**

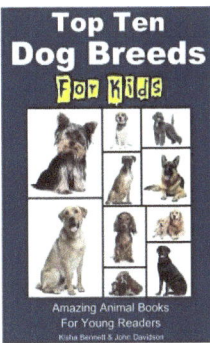
**Top Ten Dog Breeds For Kids**
Amazing Animal Books For Young Readers
Kisha Bennett & John Davidson

**German Shepherds**
Dog Books for Kids
K. Bennett

**Bulldogs**
Dog Books for Kids
K. Bennett

**Dachshund**
Dog Books for Kids
K. Bennett

**Poodles**
Dog Books for Kids
K. Bennett

**Labrador Retrievers**
Dog Books for Kids
K. Bennett

**Rottweilers**
Dog Books for Kids
K. Bennett

**Boxers**
Dog Books for Kids
K. Bennett

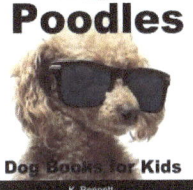

**Golden Retrievers**
Dog Books for Kids
K. Bennett

**Puppies**
Dog Books For Kids
Amazing Animal Books
By John Davidson

**Beagles**
Dog Books for Kids
K. Bennett

**Yorkshire Terriers**
Dog Books for Kids
K. Bennett

**Dogs Top Ten Dog Breeds For Kids**
Amazing Animal Books For Young Readers
Zahra Jazeel & John Davidson

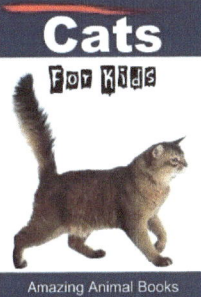
**Cats For Kids**
Amazing Animal Books For Young Readers
K. Bennett & John Davidson

**Foxes For Kids**
Amazing Animal Books For Young Readers
Zahra Jazeel & John Davidson

**Wolves For Kids**
Amazing Animal Books For Young Readers
By John Davidson and Virginia Fidler

**Monkeys**

Amazing Animal Books
For Young Readers
By John and
Annalee Davidson

**Whales**

Amazing Animal Books
For Young Readers
By John Davidson

**Kittens**

Amazing Animal Books
For Young Readers
By John Davidson

**Meerkats**
For Kids

Amazing Animal Books
For Young Readers
John Davidson and Lisa Barry

**Elephants**
For Kids

Amazing Animal Books
For Young Readers
Kim Chase & John Davidson

**Big Mammals of Yellowstone**
For Kids

Amazing Animal Books
For Young Readers
By John Davidson

**Big Cats**
For Kids

Amazing Animal Books
For Young Readers
By John Davidson

**My First Book About Pandas**

Amazing Animal Books
By Annalee and John Davidson
BEST

Children's Picture Books

**Chinchillas**

Amazing Animal Books
For Young Readers
John Davidson and Jamie Rhynsburger

**Beavers**
For Kids

Amazing Animal Books
For Young Readers
By J Davidson

**Bees**

Amazing Animal Books
For Young Readers
By J Davidson and Jennifer Lejeune

**Animals of Australia**
For Kids

Amazing Animal Books
For Young Readers
By John Davidson
and Shawn Vincent Wilson

**Frogs**
For Kids

Amazing Animal Books
For Young Readers
By John Davidson

**My First Book About Frogs**

Amazing Animal Books
By John Davidson

Children's Picture Books

**Tigers**
For Kids

Amazing Animal Books
For Young Readers
Kim Chase & John Davidson

**Scorpions**
For Kids

Amazing Animal Books
For Young Readers
John Davidson

**Snakes**

Amazing Animal Books
For Young Readers
By John Davidson and Nadine Thele

**Animals of Africa**
For Kids

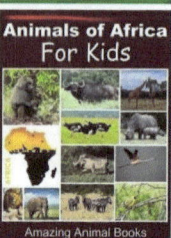

Amazing Animal Books
For Young Readers
Steve Muturi & John Davidson

**Dinosaurs**

For Kids

Amazing Animal Books
For Young Readers
By John Davidson

**Sharks**
For Kids

Amazing Animal Books
For Young Readers
By John Davidson

**Spiders**

For Kids

Amazing Animal Books
For Young Readers
By John Davidson

**Giant Panda Bears**

Amazing Animal Books
For Young Readers
By John Davidson

**Giraffes**
For Kids

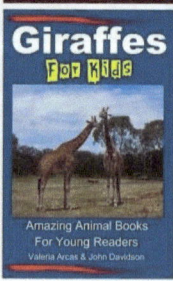

Amazing Animal Books
For Young Readers
Valeria Arcas & John Davidson

**Eagles**

For Kids

Amazing Animal Books
For Young Readers
Nicholas Williams  & John Davidson

**Bears**
For Kids

Amazing Animal Books
For Young Readers
Zahra Jazeel & John Davidson

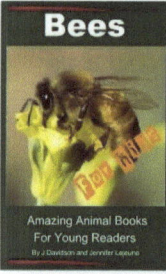

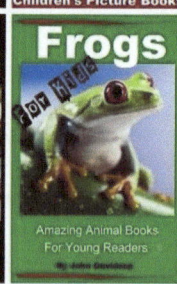

---

Our books are available at

1. Amazon.com

2. Barnes and Noble

3. Itunes

4. Kobo

5. Smashwords

6. Google Play Books

# Download Free Books!
# http://MendonCottageBooks.com

# Publisher

JD-Biz Corp

P O Box 374

Mendon, Utah 84325

http://www.jd-biz.com/

www.ingramcontent.com/pod-product-compliance
Lightning Source LLC
Chambersburg PA
CBHW050850290526
45792CB00002B/601